THE WORLD CHANGER'S HANDBOOK

A YOUNG PERSON'S GUIDE TO CREATING AN IMPACTFUL LIFE

ZACHARY JONES

Thank you, Randy Kinzly, for changing the way I saw the world.

CONTENTS

ACKNOWLEDGMENTS

Thank you to my early readers, Sophia Sadock, Amy Caldicott, Connie Bugbee, Joanna Jones, my amazing editor Ann Maynard, and the Horn Program in Entrepreneurship for inspiring me to be a world changer.

If you've found this book, you probably don't need much convincing. You live in an incredible time, but your situation is far from perfect. There is violence, hatred, poverty and disease throughout the world. Countless problems remain unsolved.

Most people will cross their fingers and hope someone else takes care of the issues plaguing our world. I hope you will take the bolder path to stand up and start making the change you need to see.

I've experienced the power that one small moment can have. A tiny act of courage can ignite a lifetime of service. A sixty-second pitch could launch your career as a social entrepreneur. One realization can change who you are as a person.

I live for these small steps that can change our lives, and eventually, the world. This book is about the habits and insights that have fueled my fire.

This is for those who see a brighter future and are ready to make it happen.

1

A CALL TO ACTION

"Whether you think you can, or think you can't—you're right."
— Henry Ford

Belief

The journey

All Journeys Start with Belief

Belief is the most valuable currency you have. Strangely, it's worth nothing until you give it away.

I remember the life-changing moment when someone gave me belief. I was 15 years old, wearing a sweaty practice jersey and frustrated that no one else on my basketball team knew our plays. My coach, Randy Kinzly, pulled me aside to tell me that I wasn't just a basketball player, I was a leader. Suddenly, I was a part of something bigger. Watching my teammates struggle was inexcusable. It was my job as a leader to step in and help.

I never saw myself the same way again.

Before that moment, I showed up to the game and I hoped my shots went in. I was just one of five players out on the court. Each of us trying to do our best, please our parents and impress our classmates.

After I became a leader, I showed up early and took ownership of everyone knowing our plays. I brought a new energy to practice and worked hard every single day. That was the best team I've ever played on. We weren't the most talented group, but we all had each other's backs.

At the end of the day, high school basketball means very little, but the lesson I learned that day changed the way I saw the world forever. It started me on a journey that I plan to continue for the rest of my life.

Staying on the sidelines won't make our world a better place. We need people to believe in their power to make a difference.

If you've never felt like this before, keep reading and know that I believe in you. I trust you to pass this belief on to someone who needs it. All the while, it will spread like a flame—burning within you, and lighting up those around you.

Rediscovering Your Ambition

You started out with big dreams to be an astronaut, a doctor or the president, but over the years you've become "more realistic." Being comfortable with your own ambition is not easy. In fact, most people become so uncomfortable that they stop thinking big.

"Forget your dream job; you're lucky to get any job these days." That's the prevailing narrative we hear in the media, and it's a sad reality that I see played out every day. I've talked to high school students who are already resigned to that fact that they will dislike their job. They've been taught to forget about passion and grind through school so they can make more money. Why settle so soon?

What happened to your dreams of changing the world?

Maybe your dreams have been scared out of you. Maybe when you shared your ambitions with your friends they gave you a funny look and called you a "try-hard." They made you feel weird because you had big dreams and they did not. You stood out because you dared when no one else did.

Even if your friends say you're weird, they secretly admire your drive. Maybe by sharing your dreams, for the first time in years, a friend will believe he should have a dream again.

It's time to get comfortable with your ambitions. Chase your dream, share it with others and take the little steps to make it happen.

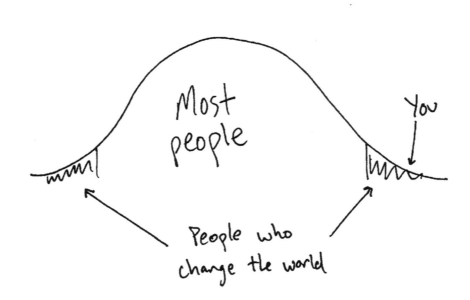

Three Facts about Life

Fact 1: Most people are average
Fact 2: Average people don't change the world
Fact 3: You are not average

Most of the people you encounter won't share your drive. When you talk about your dream, they might even discourage you. We've all heard, "I wanted to be that, too," from the person who loves the environment, but became a banker because he couldn't imagine a career in sustainability that made "enough" money.

"All advice is autobiographical."
– Austin Kleon

Most dreamers are persuaded by average people to believe that their ambitions are unrealistic. That's not you. You are not average and you *are* going to change the world.

Creativity Is Fragile

"Those who say it cannot be done, should not interrupt those doing it."
— Chinese Proverb

It's easy for creativity to dwindle. Maybe it happened when you did wacky experiments at home, or you tried coloring outside the lines in art class.

One of those days, someone probably said you were doing it wrong. They wanted to contain you, to make sure you fit the mold. They did their best to ensure you didn't stand out.

Over the course of our lives, well-meaning people slowly kill our creativity. They want us to follow the rules, get a safe job and have a normal life. They don't know any better. They don't realize that this advice has created a world of apathetic, uninspired followers.

You aren't average or normal. Why would you ever want to be?

The challenge now is to revitalize your creativity. It was never gone, just suppressed.

Exercise your creative muscle and don't let anyone take away your voice. We need your unique contribution now more than ever.

It's on Us to Create Change

There are a million reasons why the status quo is fine. That's why it takes a bold individual to spearhead a movement. Before we see world-changing innovations take off, we're going to need more people to take a step into the unknown and make it happen.

"Fitting in is a short-term strategy that gets you nowhere.
Standing out is a long-term strategy that takes guts and produces results."
— Seth Godin

Everyone knows someone who has been killed or seriously injured in a car crash. Yet, self-driving cars, the very ones that could save tens of thousands of lives each year, are met with huge resistance. Most people oppose change even in the face of a lifesaving upside.

Where are world changers supposed to come from? They aren't bred in schools or universities. They aren't coming from big companies either. Our society fails to encourage world changers. Civilization wasn't built to create people who change the status quo. It's on us to solve the countless problems facing our world. We have to build the next generation of leaders to take us into a brighter future.

The capital exists to invest in new projects. Big companies are starving for innovation. There are plenty of good ideas out there. There just aren't enough people willing to pursue them. I think you're up for the task.

The Best Time to Take Your First Step

"Later" means never and "someday" doesn't come.

We all know people who are "waiting for the right time" to start their project. Newsflash: people who wait for the right time to start never get anything done!

There will always be evidence suggesting that right now is the wrong time to start. The good news is you only need one ounce of hope to take the first step. You can make an outline for a blog post in five minutes. You can sketch out a website idea while you wait for your lunch. You can record a YouTube video on your phone on your walk to class. None of these actions require you to quit your job. They just require you to take one small step in the right direction.

"If I get an idea, I immediately take a step forward and see how that feels.
If it feels good, I take another step. If it feels bad, I step back."
— Yvon Chouinard

My hunch is that once you take a step, your fear will shrink and your momentum will grow. There's excitement in dipping a toe into the unknown.

What if You Had No Fear?

For two years I helped organize a speaker series at the University of Delaware where we brought in dozens of entrepreneurs to share their stories. We had public company CEOs, early startup founders and massively successful immigrants.

I'll never forget what one speaker said when asked the question, "What advice would you give to college students interested in entrepreneurship?"

"Stop being so afraid."

She wasn't alone in giving this advice. I've heard this message echoed dozens of times by the hundreds of speakers I've heard in the past four years. As humans, we systematically spend too much time thinking about what could go wrong. You are not a reckless person. You are competent and caring. If you try something new and it doesn't work, life will go on. You'll be better for it.

> *"Everything you've ever wanted is on the other side of fear."*
> *— George Addair*

There's a biological reason why we're fearful of going against the status quo. Standing out used to be life-threatening behavior. Being alone in a tribal society meant you were defenseless and vulnerable. That's why we're terrified of public speaking. Being one person standing in front of many activates that biological fear.

Times have changed. Survival is no longer determined by your ability to fit in. Too much fitting in is how we got into this mess of pollution, corruption and hatred. It's time for people like us to stand out and start making change.

"It is no measure of health to be well adjusted to a profoundly sick society."
— Jiddu Krishnamurti

We're All Entrepreneurs

Entrepreneurship is a scary word. It sounds risky, technological and profit-driven. However, that's not the point at all. We're all entrepreneurial every day. Entrepreneurship is about capturing and delivering value from a new idea.

That's what a basketball coach does when she draws up a new play. That's what a teacher does when he teaches a lesson using music instead of a textbook. That's what a leader does when she has to rally her team around a new project.

It's what you have to do when you see a problem that no one else recognizes.

How Big Is the World?

There's been a lot of talk about changing the world. Let's clarify the scale we're talking about.

The world is a collection of human beings. Changing the world is simple. All you have to do is change one of the human beings. You can empower her, give her belief, understand her and connect her with others. One by one, these actions all change the world.

A great teacher creates world changers. While she may only have 20 kids in her class, if she can empower them to make the change they want to see, there will be a domino effect. One of those students might go on to found an organization that builds hundreds of homes for the homeless. Another student might become a nurse who sets an example for the whole hospital with her devotion to patient care. While the classroom may seem small, the potential for impact is world-changingly large.

Never underestimate the power of the ripple effect.

What Will You Create?

The barriers to starting are lower than ever before. If you have something valuable to say, the power of the internet can help you reach an audience instantly.

A good friend of mine published his first blog post on the free platform Medium.com. Tens of thousands of people read it because it was a great article full of useful advice. He reached thousands without any costs other than his connection to the internet.

You don't have to spend any money to make a flyer on Google Docs, or create a Facebook group for people who believe in your cause.

There are countless free ways to make change. So what will you create?

start a Facebook group

make a flyer in Google docs

Start an email list on Mailchimp

Free ways to take your first step

host a live meetup

record a video on YouTube

invite people to a slack channel

blog on medium.com

SOME SAY ONE PERSON CAN'T CHANGE THE WORLD. THAT'S CRAZY. ONE PERSON IS THE ONLY WAY ANY CHANGE CAN START.

What We've Covered

- The first step in any journey is belief
- It's up to us to build a brighter future, so let's stop waiting
- Small actions change the world
- Never underestimate the power of the ripple effect

2

YOUR ARENA FOR IMPACT

You know you want to make an impact, but you're not sure where to start. Should you volunteer this weekend? Should you start a social venture? Should you change your major? These are all valid questions, but before we go any further, we need to get clear on something else first: Who do you care to serve?

"I like to help people," is a phrase I hear often. While this is kind, it's hard to focus when your target audience is every person on the planet. In order to start making your impact count, you need to determine for whom you want to create value.

Once you choose your audience, then you need to define the scope. The beautiful thing about making change is that you can set up the constraints however you want. There is no rubric to follow. You can map out your impact however you see fit.

Who Do You Care to Serve?

"Serve those who serve others."
— Simon Sinek

Simon Sinek, orator of the famous TED Talk "Start With Why," tells a story of talking to an ER doctor serving overseas with the Air Force. He asks him, "Do you get the same fulfillment working at an ER in the States as working with the Air Force in Afghanistan?" The doctor answers along the lines of, "No, not even close. Most of the people that come to the ER in the States are drunks or idiots. No one serving in the Air Force is drunk or an idiot. They want to serve our country."

Your calling is to serve people you care about serving.

I've started to realize this for myself. I don't want to create my best work for selfish people. It's not rewarding to help someone become more narcissistic and self-absorbed. Imagine looking back after 30 years and seeing that your work has made greedy people richer. That doesn't sound like the impact our world needs.

As you map out your next steps, you have the power to choose for whom you will create value. Since you have a choice, you might as well make it a good one. Create value for people you care to serve. That decision changes the world.

Foresight: Deliberately Choosing Your Path

When you're starting something new, there are dozens of paths you can take. You get to choose who you're going to serve, where you're going to be and when you're going to work. There are no wrong decisions, but when you're mapping out a project, a club, or a career, keep in mind that you need to look down the road to make the best choice for you.

Seth Godin uses a Monopoly metaphor: Don't pick Park Place and then complain that it's too expensive to build houses. Don't pick Oriental Avenue and complain that rent is too low so you need dozens of people to land on you.

When we look at potential careers, we have to ask these important questions about what our lives would be like if we pick a certain job. Coding is great because you can do it from anywhere. You can develop software at home, in the Tropics, or at a coffee shop. The same is true for writing. Management doesn't work that way. You probably have to be in the office to be a manager. Unless you can manage virtual teams, then you can work from anywhere with that, too!

It isn't about the discipline you choose; it's about the path you take within that discipline. Foresight means listening to those who have gone before you. Look at their lives, ask them questions and choose a path that aligns with your values.

The Fast Track to Unhappiness

People become unhappy when they have incompatible goals. If you want lots of time to pursue extracurricular activities, that might not be compatible with a rigorous major and going to the bar five nights per week. If you want to work on Wall Street, that goal might not be compatible with finding deep meaning in your work.

I'm not here to say which goals are more desirable than others, but some goals don't play well together. It takes foresight and prioritization to know what's best for you. Are your goals in alignment?

Take Control of Other's Expectations

I used to respond to emails as fast as possible. I had notifications on so I knew the minute something arrived in my inbox. It was stressful, but I felt like people would be annoyed if I wasn't quick to respond.

My assumption was wrong. I've since stopped checking my email after a certain hour of the night and don't check it in the morning until I've gotten up and eaten breakfast. Now, I'm happier, less stressed and the world is still spinning!

"Test assumptions before condemning yourself to more misery."
— Tim Ferriss

There are small ways you can change expectations so that you're not a slave to work. When you respond to an email at 1:00 a.m. it gives others the expectation that you're available in the middle of the night. If you don't want to be checking email in the middle of the night, don't respond to any emails then. Empower others to make decisions or at least train them to wait until a decent hour to expect a response from you.

If you don't take control, then you will fall victim to others' wants. Soon, you'll be enabling their career rather than living your calling. Managing these expectations will help you craft a path you love.

Playing on Your Own Terms

The Romans were the greatest empire of the ancient world. For centuries they fended off barbarian attacks and maintained their dominance of the Mediterranean. Rome was the eternal city. They came close to defeat many times, but no general ever gave them so much trouble as Hannibal Barca.

The Carthaginian commander terrorized Roman armies with his strategic prowess. He offered them one of the most devastating defeats ever: the Battle of Cannae. Military strategists still study this event today, as it's gone down in history as one of the greatest examples of tactical brilliance.

Rome had the largest and best-trained army in the Western world, so Hannibal had to win by thinking differently. In a head-to-head battle, Rome would have been the victor, therefore Hannibal had to fight on his own terms to neutralize Rome's massive numerical advantage.

Hannibal used mountain passes, rivers, hills and forests to his benefit. He always had a trick up his sleeve that gave his army the upper hand in battle. He forced the Romans to play on his terms, not theirs.

The only way to take down a giant is to play on a battlefield where the giant's size is not a factor.

The same goes for the impact you seek to make. You don't have the resources of a large organization, so it's best that you start small. A nationwide charity doesn't have the close bonds you've built within your community. You are the better player in that small arena.

You can start with serving a free meal at your local YMCA on the first Monday of every month. The arena may be small, but it's yours and it matters.

Smart People Call Disadvantages "Design Decisions"

How you view something and how others view it completely depends on how you present the information. While you may think it's a disadvantage that you don't have a mass-manufacturing process, turn that into a design decision and sell "hand-crafted" pottery. The things you view as bad can be spun into positive attributes that differentiate you.

Not mass-produced = handcrafted
No big factory = small-batch

The hardest essay to write is the one when the teacher says you can write about whatever you want. This is because there are no constraints. There is no place for you to start! There are millions of possibilities and none of them are right. Similarly, the hardest products to sell are those without any constraints. They're trying to be everything for everyone.

Lack of constraints = lack of focus

If you're designing for everyone, you're designing for no one. Say you have a day job, but your passion is running workshops to help people learn to code. You physically can't hold workshops from 9-5 during the week because you're working. Instead of viewing this as a big problem that makes you worse than your competitors, simply accept this as a constraint. Then find a target market who would appreciate attending coding sessions on nights and weekends. Your target market might be corporate employees who are thinking about switching careers into a more technical field. Since your target market works during the day, you HAVE to hold your workshops on nights and weekends. Now, when someone asks why you hold your workshops on Thursday nights and Saturday mornings, you can say that it was a design decision. That's when your target market wants to attend.

Thing you don't want to do = constraint → find people who don't care about that constraint → now, constraint = design decision

Once you can set up your constraints, you can realistically start to explore your calling.

Leveraging Student Connections

I'm a strong believer in leverage. I want to use my brief time on this planet as meaningfully as possible. When I was a sophomore and junior in college, I realized the biggest impact I could have on the world at that time was through leading the Entrepreneurship Club.

> *"Give me a lever long enough and a fulcrum on which to place it, and I shall move the world."*
> *— Archimedes*

It may not seem like a college club would change the world, but never underestimate the power of a community. Before finding our club, entrepreneurial students felt like misfits. Without support, their passion may have faded or their creativity may have dwindled. Once they discovered our meetings, they suddenly felt like other people understood them.

The club gave motivated people a place to share ideas and help each other. I'm confident that in ten years many previous members will be wildly successful and remember their experience with the Entrepreneurship Club as a formative time period.

Your Unique Situation

Everyone is in a unique situation to make a change. The hardest part is recognizing all of the skills you take for granted and finding the right place to apply your wisdom.

It's easy to feel like constraints limit your ability to contribute, but that's not the point. No matter what your constraints are, you can define an audience you care about and start making your impact. Even if you can only commit one hour per month to tutor a girl interested in a STEM field, you're still making an impact! While it might feel like one hour a month is a small contribution, focusing on your cause and your audience means you will be more likely to spread the word about it.

When you talk to your co-workers, you can tell them about this new tutoring program. Maybe two other scientists from your company sign up on your recommendation. Through your 15-minute conversation over lunch, you've tripled your impact on the organization!

You have existing skills and a unique perspective. If you focus, you will see you're positioned perfectly to make an impact. No matter how small your arena might be, you can start serving today.

What We've Covered

- Define an audience you care to serve
- Have foresight so you can deliberately choose your path
- Play on your own terms and control expectations
- Turn constraints into advantages
- Leverage your unique situation
- No matter where you are, with the right focus you can make change

3

INSTEAD OF "PASSION"

Here are four alternative ways to think about the burning question of "What's your passion?"

*"The two most important days in your life are the day you are born
and the day you find out why."*
— Mark Twain

These ideas might help you pick a college, a major, an internship, a job, a service group, or they might even inspire you to start your own organization!

Stop Searching and Start Listening

To search for your calling implies that you're currently devoid of meaning. Searching for happiness implies that it lives somewhere else. We spend a lot of time searching for these things, but I believe that both are already inside us.

Instead of taking quizzes, googling careers and searching the outside world, what if you looked deeper within yourself?

Threads of purpose already exist in your life. Dig into that feeling by asking yourself, "Why?" Why is this enjoyable? Why am I excited for this and dreading that?

Get in touch with yourself to discover the things that light you up.

Take time to reflect each day and you won't have to go searching for purpose. You'll realize it's been inside you all along.

Stop searching and start listening to your life.

Don't Follow Your Passion; Follow Your Contribution

Most of us have no idea what we're going to do in life. Advice to "follow your passion" doesn't help much. Most people have countless passions, but it's unclear which to pursue. Passions can be self-serving, or not valuable to the outside world. There must be a better way to think about it.

Ben Horowitz is a founding partner of Andreessen Horowitz, a venture capital firm that rethinks how to grow startup companies. When I've felt stuck over the years, I think back to Ben's advice from his commencement speech at Columbia University: "Don't follow your passion. Follow your contribution."

While subtle, this distinction is critical to your fulfillment with your work. When you're improving the lives of others, you enjoy work more. Passion is about doing something that makes you happy. Contribution is about helping others in a meaningful way.

I'd never heard this advice, but it turns out Horowitz wasn't alone in his thinking. Tony Robbins is a life coach and self-help guru who echoes this sentiment in his own words. He says suffering stems from a "me-centered" view of the world. When you feel bad, you're worried about yourself and the problems you have.

Tony says happiness comes from a focus on the outside world. You can't be angry when you're feeling grateful and generous. You can't be bitter when you're putting a smile on a young child's face. When we help others, our worries about ourselves disappear. That's why following your contribution will lead to a happier and more rewarding place than following your passion.

> *"If you want to lift yourself up, lift up someone else."*
> — Booker T. Washington

Search for opportunities to contribute your authentic self to the world. Find the ways in which you can add value to other people's lives. Follow this contribution and you can finally stop worrying about this elusive thing we call "passion." It's fine that you don't know what your passion is. Keep contributing to the world and you'll be on the right track.

Your Unique Gift

How do you move past settling for a good job and discover your true calling? Yes, you're good at numbers, so someone said you'd make a good accountant or banker. But that isn't a calling. Those are good jobs, but they aren't making an emotional impact on someone's life. So what is your gift?

Phillip McKernan is an author, speaker and personal coach who helps people wrestle with this very question. His solution to this problem is cleaner and more enlightening than any I've heard.

He says your gift is: *"Your innate ability to move the needle emotionally for somebody else. To show them and let them know that they matter."*

Here's an example to make this more clear: Phillip's wife had a great accounting job in the corporate world. She performed highly because she was smart and hard-working. It was clear that she was executing her talent, but her work wasn't energizing. It was a great job, but it was far from a calling. She wasn't relieving any meaningful pain for her clients; thus, she lacked any emotional connection with the work.

To find her gift, she had to dig back further into her own struggles. Now she works in women empowerment and the energy she's found from working with her clients is unlike anything she ever felt working as an accountant.

Listen to your feelings. Maybe you have to dig deep to find this pain, or maybe it's immediately obvious. Either way, once you discover it, you will have no choice but to pursue it. You've felt alone and disconnected at some point in your life, but now you will help people experiencing those same emotions. You will let them know that they're not alone and that you understand them. There is nothing more powerful than making someone feel understood.

Sharing Your Truth

Your truth is your ability to change the world. It's the story you need to tell. It's driven by seeing something that others aren't appreciating. When a big company seeks to build a factory on a beloved nature preserve, your impact is to tell the truth about what's happening.

You share your truth to let others know you see the world like they do. You share your truth to show someone they're not alone. That is the essence of change. Loneliness hurts, but your small connection may be all someone needs in order to begin pulling himself out of the darkness.

The truth I need to tell is that you aren't confined to the system. You don't need another credential before you're allowed to make an impact. I want to be there for all the misfits who felt they were too daring to belong. You belong here and we're ready for you to start changing the world.

What We've Covered

- Stop searching for passion and start listening to your life
- Don't follow your passion; follow your contribution
- Your unique gift is to make an emotional difference in someone's life
- Share your truth with the world

4

STARTING SMALL, BUT MEANINGFUL

"To be sure, a human being is a finite thing, and his freedom is restricted.
It is not freedom from conditions, but freedom to take a stand toward the conditions."
— Viktor Frankl

The conditions aren't perfect. They never will be. What is perfect is the fact that you can stand up and make them better. The choice is yours, but I know you're up for it.

It's overwhelming to think about all of the problems in the world and how many great people are already working hard to solve them. None of those things matter. If you're feeling that this is all too much, read the next section. It's just what you need to hear.

You don't have to feel ready to change the world. You just have to be willing to try.

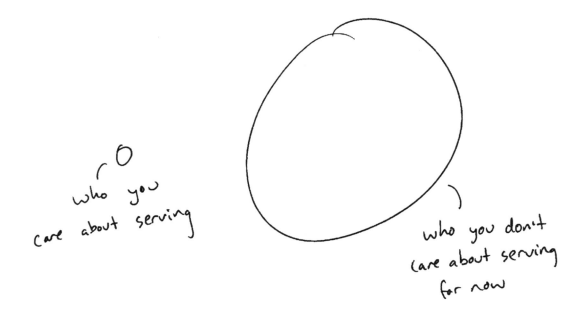

Starting with an Audience of Ten

The more specific your audience is, the easier it will be to start making progress. Maybe you're focused on college students who major in engineering and want to apply their skills to help a non-profit. Perhaps your target customers are stay-at-home parents with kids aged 2–5 living in apartments who want fun meals to cook with their children.

There's no right or wrong here, but you need to know.

It's important to define your audience, because then you know who you can NOT care about. There are only a few people who you want to reach at first. All the other people are a distraction from the ten people who truly matter when you start.

Say you've built a Facebook group for engineering students to find technical work for non-profits. If a marketing major complains that you don't have any jobs for them, that's okay! It might feel bad to turn that person away, but that's not who it's for right now.

When you're small and beginning a new project, you need all the focus you can get.

Making an Impact Starts with Caring

Change starts by caring about something bigger than yourself. Maybe it's empowering teens, feeding the hungry or making healthcare accessible to all. The best reason to take action is because you care deeply about the problem you're solving.

> *"It's hard to do a really good job on anything you don't think about in the shower."*
> *— Paul Graham*

Fame and recognition are a distraction from the problem you're solving. Caring means that you're willing to solve the problem before you have a title, before it's profitable and before it's "your job." The funny thing is, the more you care, the more likely you are to find that a job creates itself.

As a freshman at University of Delaware, I cared deeply about the admissions process. I had just gone on 20 tours before picking my college and I knew they could be more engaging. Recognizing this opportunity, my friend and I started organizing volunteers to meet with accepted high school seniors over lunch. Current students gave prospective students a personal look into campus life while sharing a meal in the dining hall. We started and ran this program for free every day for nearly three months. The following spring, when the admission season rolled around, the office hired us as student workers! We cared about creating a better touring process and it eventually turned into a job for both of us.

Your Fear of Sharing is Selfish

Too often I hear from people who have a great idea, but don't want to share it with the public. They're typically scared of it being stolen, or not receiving proper credit.

"Stolen" gets a bad rep and credit is a commodity.

If you need credit, write a textbook. When you have an idea that's generous and helpful, let it run free. The credit will come later. Holding onto a valuable idea is selfish.

When Alicia Garza, Opal Tometi and Patrisse Cullors started the Black Lives Matter movement, did they start it to get credit? No. They started because they wanted to spread an idea and change a conversation.

"You can't use up creativity. The more you use, the more you have."
– Maya Angelou

Not receiving credit is scary. Especially when you believe you just created your best work. But I've learned that work constantly gets better. I always feel like I just wrote my best blog post, and I'll never create something that good again. Then, a couple of weeks later, I make something better.

As long as you plan on writing more, sharing more and creating more, this fear should not paralyze you. The feeling is a good sign that you're on the right track and you're getting better. Maintain a habit of producing new things and sharing them with the world and you will continue to improve. Sharing doesn't mean a blast to all of your Facebook friends. Just create a place to post your ideas and let those who matter know where to find them. For me, it's my blog. Most of my friends aren't aware it exists, but the people who matter know where to find it.

If you hoard your ideas, you're missing the opportunity to share something that could change lives. Be generous and share your brilliance with us.

Perfectionism is Procrastination

Perfectionism is slowing you down and distracting you from the real work. It's a way of procrastinating while looking productive.

So why do we become perfectionists in the first place?

Fear.

We're scared that our work isn't good enough. We're scared of being done because done is so permanent. Done means that it's ready for criticism and that's scary.

Change is never perfect. Your time is too valuable to be spent trying to make it so.

You have big things to accomplish and being perfect is certainly not one of them.

Anything you create will have some flaws. But that doesn't matter. Did your grandparents shun your third grade artwork because it wasn't perfect? No. To them it was meaningful.

Your job is not to create a perfect product. It's to create things for people that move the needle emotionally. Let your generosity and kindness shine through. Anyone who hates your imperfections doesn't matter anyway. Those aren't the kind of people you want to serve.

GENEROSITY DOESN'T HAVE TO BE PERFECT.

Join Me on a Journey

Your improvement and evolution are important parts of the process. When consumers want a painting with no story, they buy it from Wal-Mart. What's interesting is that many consumers prefer art with a story behind it. They want to buy from a local artist who started out in a high school art show and has evolved into a great painter. If you refuse to release work because you're waiting for perfection, you'll never get the opportunity to share your story.

When I started my blog, I wrote this:

"Join me on a journey about creative expression. This is a challenge for me to put my thoughts, opinions and art out into the world. It's scary stepping out to do something creative. We're not used to going off the map.

I invite you to come along as I start my daily blog where I share my thoughts, observations and inspiration. Thanks for being here."

Feel free to take this and use it at the beginning of your projects. You don't need to have it all figured out. All you need to have is the courage to put your ideas into the world and the curiosity to keep looking for beauty.

"It's scary, it might not work, but that's why it's fun."

Join me on a journey

Zachary Jones

Butterflies and Fear

When you're scared, you're motivated by fear.

When you're excited, you're motivated by ambition and drive.

The strange thing is, they feel almost the same.
The butterflies in your stomach could be flapping their wings out of fear
that they'll never escape,
or out of joy that it's finally their time to shine

What We've Covered

- Decide who you don't want to serve
- Making an impact starts with caring
- Your fear of sharing is selfish
- Don't procrastinate by waiting for perfection
- Your evolution is part of the beauty

5

CREATING YOUR HABIT

Small actions will move you forward in a meaningful way.

There is no recess period where we all pause life to make change. It's way harder than that. You need to make a conscious commitment to show up and do something that matters.

It may not catch on right away, but if you care enough to share something generous every day, it will change the world.

"Most people overestimate what they can do in one year and underestimate what they can do in ten years."
— Bill Gates

Testing the Waters with a Habit of Creation

I don't recommend that you quit your job, drop out of school or do anything drastic when you're starting a journey like this. It would be great if your side hustle turned into a living, but until you have evidence that a project will sustain you and make you happy, keep it on the side. There are dozens of ways to test the waters before spending any money on something unproven. The most powerful of these methods is building a daily habit of creation.

Create for yourself at first. Before you test whether the market likes your project, you have to test if you care enough to show up every day and make it. It might take a year of hard work every day before people start to notice anyway. It's important to enjoy the process of creation because most of the time, that's all you have.

If you want to be a cartoon artist, don't wait for permission to be published. Start an Instagram account and share a cartoon every day. You're not going to get paid for them, but you're going to gain something more valuable than money: trust. If you can't bear the thought of making cartoons and not getting paid, it's not your calling.

The cornerstone of this strategy is the connection that you're building with your audience. There's something powerful about people trusting you to post your work every day. You'll also become a better cartoonist by building this habit.

"Diligence is the mother of good luck."
— *Benjamin Franklin*

You can draw one picture, come up with one idea or give one compliment today, but the thought of doing it every day is dizzying. That's a silly way to look at life. The whole doesn't matter right now. All that matters is the first step you take today.

An average person walks 110,000 miles in their lifetime. That's a staggering number, but on a daily basis, it's just over 3 miles each day. Is that too much to ask?

The Power of a Daily Habit

"You will never change your life until you change something you do daily."
— *Mike Murdock*

Two years ago I decided that I wanted to become a better writer. Everything I read said the only way to get better at writing was to sit down and do it! Reluctantly, I started typing away until I had a somewhat cohesive article that I published on the free blogging platform, Medium.com. I did this about once a week, sometimes more, but usually less. A year passed and I had published about 30 articles. I felt more comfortable writing, but I was still far from where I wanted to be. I had accomplished a realistic goal, but I hadn't gotten the results I'd hoped for.

"The greater danger for most of us lies not in setting our aim too high and falling short;
but in setting our aim too low, and achieving our mark."
— Michelangelo

After hearing Seth Godin's advice to start a daily blog more times than I can count, I finally did on September 14, 2016. There was no more compromising. I had to finish an article every day and post it online. The requirement to post something every day changed the way I thought about my schedule. I needed to wake up earlier to write. I needed to have ideas, opinions and observations to write about. I started being more observant, taking more notes and seeing inspiration in everything. Most importantly, I started viewing myself as a writer.

After just four months of writing daily, I improved more than I did in a year and a half of writing sporadically.

No matter what your goal is, you can make progress every day. Say you want to become a better painter, but you're only in the studio three times per week. During the other days you can collect inspiration, make sketches and visualize your future work. There is inspiration everywhere and countless stories are waiting to be told.

The important shift is when you go from being "a student who paints" to being "a painter who goes to school." Adopting the lens of the artist changes the way you see the world. It's inspired. It's creative and it matters. Create your daily habit and start making the impact you've always wanted to see.

Don't Look for Time; Make It

There are plenty of reasons why you're too busy to do anything remarkable. There's always more to read, watch and consume. You're never going to stumble upon free time. If you truly care about change, you need to make the time.

If you don't carve out time, it will disappear. It's a sad fact, but we can either mope about it or we can work with it.

> *"Life is what happens while you're too busy making other plans."*
> *— John Lennon*

Most people say they don't have time to read. Really? How many minutes does it take to read a few pages of your book? I'm sure you could stay up two minutes later and read three pages. Or better yet, wake up two minutes earlier and read three pages.

Commit to that time. No compromises. You're going to read a few pages each night or morning. Or both!

My guess is that you'll realize you have a few free minutes and can read at least 10 pages per day. Make that your new goal and then you're on pace to read a book in a month! Not bad. Much better than saying, "I don't have time to read."

Make time for the things that matter. Stay focused on the impact you seek to make. Show up on a consistent basis and you will slowly start to change the world.

No Inspiration Required

Do you need to be inspired in order to create?

I don't think so. What you need is more difficult to obtain than inspiration or motivation. You need discipline and honesty. The best art is that which is authentic and truthful.

Motivation might push you to create one piece, but discipline will push you to create an amazing body of work. Art is a series of small steps, not one huge leap. The boom and bust cycle of motivation is unreliable.

The hardest thing about art is getting out of the way of your own truth. Your perspective is valuable, but it's scary to share.

Do us all a favor and don't wait until you're inspired to share your truth. Be disciplined and make a habit out of sharing your view today. We appreciate it.

Discipline and honesty > inspiration

What We've Covered

- Test the waters with a habit of creation
- Daily habits fundamentally change your perspective
- Make time for the things that matter
- Discipline and honesty are more reliable than motivation

6

CONNECTING WITH YOUR PEOPLE

You have to start small—creating for yourself, your friends, and your community. But it doesn't stay small for long. This next section will explore how to grow your impact and touch more souls.

Recreating Your Best Days

What are your top five days ever?[1]

For me, other than falling in love with my girlfriend, my top five were all days in which I was surrounded by groups of world changers. Those days gave me energy. They reframed possibility and gave me the strong conviction that I could change the world.

We need time with our people or else we'll lose those feelings. We'll never know who is standing behind us as we trek into uncharted territory. The support is out there, but we need to find it.

At the end of the day we don't remember what was said. We remember how we felt. The most transformative and important experiences are those that inspire, empower and understand. You can accomplish these things through stories, activities or simply listening. Being heard and understood are emotions that very few people feel on a regular basis.

Think about your top five days and how they made you feel. Recreate those emotions for other people and you will have a huge impact on their lives.

---

[1] This is an exercise from Philip McKernan

All That Remains

I once attended a beautiful celebration of life ceremony for my grandma. Members of the immediate family shared their favorite memories between sniffling, laughter and tears.

Every memory was based on the simple gift of time. The time spent having meals together. The time spent playing games at the dining room table. The time spent reading a book to her grandkids.

It may seem like all we leave behind in this world are our physical possessions, but in fact it's quite the opposite. All that remains is the time we spent together.

Making Someone's Day

You would love to make someone's day, so why don't you do it more? It requires taking a risk. Giving a compliment could be the best part of your friend's day but it might backfire. Moments like these happen all the time. You fear speaking up because you're not sure how your words will be received.

When you feel this resistance, it's a sign you should run toward it. Go out of your way even if it's uncomfortable. Running away from these feelings is a mistake that makes everyone worse off.

Practice gratitude and appreciation. People are working hard all around us and wishing someone would speak up and give them credit.

Recognize the underappreciated worker. Go out of your way to thank an artist for her performance. Talk to the lonely person a few seats down from you. You never know whose day you might make.

Hiding in the Corners

There is always a corner of the world where you can connect with your people. There are a lot of corners in the labyrinth of life, so it's not always easy to find yours. You might search through Meetup.com groups, Facebook pages, coffee houses or Reddit threads hoping to find it.

Just know that your corner is out there. People do exist who connect with your story, but they might be hiding. In fact, they might be waiting for someone like you to come along and be bold enough to share your story first. They need someone to explain the emotion you're all feeling and unite this corner of the world in understanding each other.

They're waiting for you. So what are you waiting for?

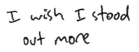

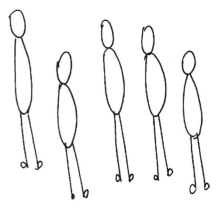

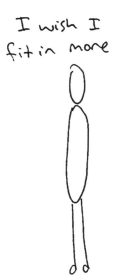

How to Stop Feeling Alone

I felt alone for years. I thought I was the only one on my team who cared, the only person interested in making change. But I was wrong. That wasn't the case at all. I was just too stuck in my own mind to realize that there was help all around me.

There are other people who understand the pain you're feeling. No matter what it is, and how unique your situation seems, it's true. I know because I went years feeling that no one could truly understand the change I wanted to make. I would bring in speakers to the Entrepreneurship Club hoping one day to find a mentor to relate to my pain. No one made the cut.

Eventually I was telling someone how 50 people spoke to the club and none were good enough. He asked, "Do you think you gave them a chance?"

That's all it took to change my mind. These people weren't lousy human beings. The problem was I never gave them a chance. It's too easy to forget that even the most outwardly different people are very similar to you. I'm still working on this flaw and seeing progress.

Lately, I've been able to connect with tribes of people that *do* understand the change I make. I'm connected with people who give me energy. I finally found a place of understanding. Not because the people were any better than before, but because I finally made myself open to connection.

Before, there was a small part of me that enjoyed being an enigma. It was satisfying that there was always something people didn't understand. I was hiding. Hiding from emotions. Hiding from meaningful connections with people experiencing the same pain.

I was going at it alone when there was support all around me if I were just willing to ask. There's a beautiful quote from Glennon Doyle Melton, author of *Love Warrior*, which reads:

"Life is not hard because you're making a mistake. Life is hard because it was designed that way. If it wasn't hard, we wouldn't need each other and needing each other is the best part of life."
— Glennon Doyle Melton

Next time you feel like you're having a tough time, let someone know. Call a friend, email a professor, or talk to a counselor. Your pain is not unique. We are all here to give and help those around us. It takes a lot of courage to ask, and it might not work the first time. But that's what makes it so valuable. Most people won't do it. You need to be vulnerable enough to make your voice heard.

What We've Covered

- Recreate your top five days for other people
- All that remains is the time we spent together
- Connecting with people requires a small risk
- Be vulnerable enough to ask for help

7

FOCUSING ON THE PROCESS

It may seem scary to start something without making a formal plan, but that's exactly what you need to do. Instead of thinking about the outcome, you need to focus on a process.

Focus on the productive activities rather than the busyness that bogs us down. Growth will come as long as you're doing great work.

YOU CAN'T CONNECT
THE DOTS LOOKING FORWARD,
YOU CAN ONLY CONNECT THEM
LOOKING BACKWARDS.
- STEVE JOBS

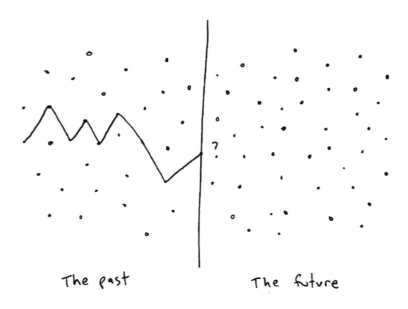

The past   The future

Busy vs. Productive

"When everyone is busy, don't expect a more productive society. Expect a frantic society."
— Jeff Davidson

Being busy is not something to be proud of. It's a badge that we wear, but one that we need to shed. I've been busy a lot, trust me. Nothing good comes out of it other than a superficial level of "success" and "importance" because your time is filled with miscellaneous activities.

My biggest breakthroughs have come when I wasn't busy.

It may not seem wise to leave open space. Sometimes it means you don't respond to an email for two days, or you don't get a perfect grade on that paper you turned in. One of the best decisions I ever made was to not schedule anything on Monday mornings in the fall of 2016. Every Monday I was free from 9:00 a.m.-12:00 p.m. My best ideas have come during those hours. In fact, this book was born out of them.

The important work is never busy work. You can hire people at minimum wage to do busy work for you. The difficult work is connecting dots that no one else can see. The difficult work is usually invisible when you're busy. Being busy fogs our minds.

Let go of busy and focus on the productive behaviors that generate results.

Don't start with a logo, don't make a website, don't form an LLC. Go test out your change in the real world. Ask to speak to a class of young people. Give a workshop for burnt-out professionals. See how your impact lands before you do the busy work of taking care of the little things.

Productive activities are testing ideas that might not work.

The Problem with Goals

Congrats! You've achieved every goal humanly possible. So, what's next?

We are taught from a young age to set ambitious goals because one day we will accomplish them and life will be great! Unfortunately, it doesn't work like that. There is a huge tendency to reset your sights every time you accomplish a goal. Once you win five games, you want to win ten games. Once you're CEO of a small company, you want to be CEO of a bigger company. Are we surprised this is our tendency in a world that always asks, "What's next?"

The problem with this model is that there's no escape. No goal is ever satisfying enough. We always want a little more, a little faster, a little bigger.

"Instead of wondering when your next vacation is, you ought to
set up a life you don't need to escape from."
— Seth Godin

Tireless pursuit of a goal keeps our minds focused on the future rather than the present. We forget to enjoy the moment because every hour only exists to serve our goal quest.

We tell ourselves the lie that if we accomplish our goals, then we'll finally be happy. But then we reset our sights and leave ourselves no room to enjoy the satisfaction of a life well-lived. Or even worse, we finally accomplish everything imaginable and realize there's no time left to appreciate the life we've created.

So are we bound to an unfulfilling wasteland of accomplished goals? Are we destined for a lackadaisical life without ambition? Nope. Fortunately, there is a way around it.

The better route is to set a goal that you can accomplish by following an enjoyable path. The only goals worth achieving are goals we would enjoy working toward. When you're thinking about starting a new project, don't think about the outcome. Think about the process that it would take to get there. The beautiful thing about process is that you can enjoy it every day.

You Don't Need a 5-Year Plan

In Nightline's famous segment from 1999, they show IDEO's design process. IDEO has designed toothbrushes, toys, trains and medical devices, but they are not experts in any one of these disciplines. Their strategy instead is to become experts in the process. The steps involve collaboration and real-world testing. It's far more effective than designing in isolation.

> *"Enlightened trial and error succeeds over the planning of the lone genius."*
> *– Peter Skillman*

The keys to the IDEO process are:

- Talk to experts
- Understand the problems
- Come up with lots of ideas
- Define goals and parameters
- Pick the best ideas
- Prototype them quickly
- Test in the real world
- Repeat

Long-term plans are often a fool's game. The better route is to try mini experiments, see how you like them and iterate from there. Start making your impact in a small way. When you call it an experiment, there's no pressure for it to work over the long term. You'll learn by interacting with the world and soon you'll be ready to make a slightly bigger impact.

Before starting my daily blog that lead to this book, I started an anonymous Instagram account sharing inspirational pictures every day. I liked the essence of sharing a powerful message, but I learned that channel didn't suit me. As a result, I started blogging and haven't looked back.

Competing with Apathy

Whenever you start something new—a blog, a social media account, a startup, a non-profit— your biggest competitor is always the same: apathy. No one knows who you are and thus they don't care about your new project yet.

The question is how do you reach new people? How do you defeat apathy?

When I was President of the Entrepreneurship Club, we wasted months pitching our club to strangers. They didn't care. They didn't want to hear from us and they sure as hell didn't want to join our club. A random pitch from a stranger rarely defeats apathy.

It was a disappointing waste of time, but a valuable lesson. We stopped doing that and shifted our focus to making our meetings great for our existing members. Oddly enough, the less we cared about recruiting new people, the more people kept coming! We focused on running engaging events and providing value to our members and the recruitment problem took care of itself. That's the secret.

The better our meetings were, the more members brought their friends. That's how the word spreads and that's how a movement starts.

Finding the Remarkable in the Mundane

How do you make something remarkable? Simple. Find the mundane and make it extraordinary. Derek Sivers was an internet entrepreneur running a company that mailed people CDs when he decided to write a quirky shipment confirmation email. It went WAY over the top in describing the hilarious intricacies of a completely fictitious CD delivery process. It was absurd, but it was remarkable. It made people smile and laugh. People told their friends, bloggers posted it online and news outlets shared the story like crazy.

Those 30 minutes he spent turning a generic email into something amazing gained him more PR than a startup budget could ever buy. When thinking about how to reach new people with your change, don't think about buying ads and doing sales calls. You want your message to spread organically through a trusted group of peers.

Did people start going to Chipotle because they saw their commercial? No, they started going because their friends said there was a fast, cheap and delicious burrito place in town that everyone needed to try.

How can you share a story that people have to retell?

What We've Covered

- Know the difference between busy and productive
- Accomplish goals by following an enjoyable path
- Practice enlightened trial and error
- Your biggest competitor is always apathy
- Find the remarkable by transforming the mundane

8

FIVE WAYS TO GET UNSTUCK

When you're absorbed in making change, it's easy to lose track of time. After hours of great work, you'll find yourself unable to focus. You've been scrolling through Facebook and you haven't responded to those critical emails. You need to write a blog post, but you have no good ideas. You've lost momentum and now you feel stuck.

Everyone has been there and there's nothing I can tell you that will make you immune to feeling stuck again in the future. What I can share are some simple strategies for moving forward when it feels like nothing's going your way.

Take a Walk Around

If you've been sitting for more than 30 minutes straight, don't get frustrated that you can't focus. We're not wired to sit down for that long and focus on one thing. It's time to stand up and walk around. Get your blood moving and come back a few minutes later with new energy. If you're stuck in a meeting, a car or an auditorium and you can't get on your feet, take a minute to relax. Roll your neck around and take some deep breaths. Release the tension in your body. When I take a deep breath after a long time working, my shoulders feel like they drop six inches.

We've all been planted on a couch, at a desk, or in a chair—after 45 minutes our brains feel fried and our eyes glaze over. Instead of beating yourself up about not being productive, just stand up and walk around.

Shower Mode

Who has their best ideas in the shower? *Everyone raises hand*

The shower is what creativity researchers call "incubation time." It's an opportunity for all the ideas that have been stuck in our heads to develop and surface. Incubation is a crucial part of the creative process, but it's a counterintuitive notion. Thinking less leads to better ideas? Huh? It's true.

When we're feeling overwhelmed, we want to go faster and be more efficient. That was a good idea in the Industrial Age when we made widgets on an assembly line, but that way of thinking doesn't help anymore. You're doing creative work now that requires focus and insight.

When we're feeling stuck, the worst thing to do is to try to jam more ideas into our brain. A better route is to take a step back and get your mind off the topic. Juggle a soccer ball, walk outside, or cook lunch. Do something that distracts your mind. Your brain is still busy, but now on a subconscious level.

Incubation time allows those brilliant ideas lurking in your subconscious to come to life. Your great ideas are in there. Make the time to go into shower mode and let them surface.

The Two Happiness Thieves

There are two thieves who routinely steal our happiness. They operate in broad daylight and there's nothing we can do right now to stop them from coming next week. All we can do is understand why they come and do our best each day to stay aware.

Most unhappiness comes from two things: hunger or exhaustion. Whenever I'm feeling frustrated or overwhelmed, one of these factors is always a big part of the equation.

When I don't get enough sleep, I'm less patient, caring and attentive. It's still possible to be happy and have a great day, but I find that I'm much less resilient. When I haven't eaten in awhile, the same things happen.

If you're not in the best mood, look to these things first.

Most unhappiness is not caused by external circumstances; it's caused by how we react to them. Get more sleep and eat better and you'll be ready to take on anything.

Changing Your Perspective

One of my favorite quotes is from Astro Teller of Google X Labs:

> *"Sometimes changing your perspective can be more powerful than being smart."*

If you're feeling stuck, find a new way to look at your problem. We call these creative lenses, a powerful, yet underutilized tool in creative problem solving. Take a fresh view from the eyes of a child, or a grandparent, or someone who doesn't speak your language.

Even better, take a look from the perspective of yourself in 10 years. What would future you say about this dilemma? Would they tell you to worry more about how your hair looks? Or would they advise you to enjoy your youth because you'll never be as young as you are today.

It's easy to feel stuck when you're ruminating on a problem for a long time. Recognize this feeling and try on a new lens.

The Labyrinth

We believe the illusion that progress is linear. "The corporate ladder." "Moving up in the ranks." After all, that's how school works. Every year, you move up one more rung.

The reality is most people have no idea where they are going. Maybe they're climbing the ladder or maybe they're just hanging on for dear life.

Successful people rarely take a straightforward path. Their journeys are littered with dead ends, failures and changed directions.

If you're ever feeling stuck, remember that success is a labyrinth, not a ladder. Don't be scared of hitting a wall. Be prepared to change directions when you do.

WARNING! YOU'RE IN A LABYRINTH. PROCEED ACCORDINGLY.

YOU WILL NEVER ESCAPE, BUT THERE ARE PLENTY OF OTHER PEOPLE HERE EAGER TO JOIN YOU. ENJOY THE JOURNEY BECAUSE ONE DAY IT WILL END. YOU'LL WISH WITH ALL YOUR MIGHT THAT YOU COULD BE STANDING RIGHT HERE AT THIS AGE AGAIN.

What We've Covered

- Take a walk every 30 minutes
- Let your mind go into shower mode
- Hunger and exhaustion make you feel more stuck
- Look at your problem from a new perspective
- Life is a labyrinth; sometimes being stuck is a sign you need to change direction

9

MORE IS NEVER THE ANSWER

We tend to think that if we can accomplish the next goal, get the next paycheck or change one more thing, then we can finally be happy. But it never works like that.

I've had to learn most of these hard lessons on my own. This section will give you a new perspective I wish I had known.

Your happiness is the essential ingredient for an impactful life. Without it, none of the achievements matter.

The Sobering Realization That You Will Never Escape You

How you feel right now—scared, nervous, wanting more—is how you will feel in the future, no matter how much outward success you find. Though your life may look different to the observer, inside you will always be the same you.

This is the most terrifying and freeing thing you will ever realize. Terrifying, because when you realize it, there is nowhere to hide. No title, amount of money or material possession will complete your being. Freeing, because you no longer have to wait to be happy. Your happiness can't be contingent on anything else. It's up to you right now to be happy.

> *"Happiness is a choice and a skill."*
> *— Naval Ravikant*

The hardest choice we have to make every single day, in every single moment, is to be happy with what we have. It's SO satisfying to pretend that when you make thousands each month everything will be fine. Maybe you pretend that you'll finally feel like enough when you become a VP at your company. Or, when you own a home your life will be complete.

We imagine that happiness is hiding right around the corner and with one more promotion we'll finally find it.

Hello
my name is: ———
AND
I'm waiting for : ———
to start being happy

Just like chasing the pot of gold at the end of a rainbow, you will keep searching endlessly for that bit of joy. When we were kids we realized the gold wasn't there. Unfortunately, life is often too brief for us to realize that the happiness we're seeking isn't hidden in accomplishments.

Happiness is in every moment. It's not something that is given to us. It's something we learn to create. Through gratitude, appreciation, mindfulness and growth we can discover happiness in everything.

The uncomfortable thing about happiness is that it's not permanent. We love "set it and forget it" products. We love to buy Amazon Prime once and not worry about paying for shipping for the whole year. Happiness doesn't work like that.

Happiness is a process.

One vacation to a third world country will not earn you a life full of appreciation. Your mindset might be different when you step back on U.S. soil, but it will fade just as fast as it came. The only way around a fleeting sense of appreciation is to maintain a daily practice. Start to develop an awareness of when you're not feeling happy.

The times when I'm taken out of the moment are often those when I'm thinking about how I need something to feel better. How I need to make more money so I can eat at restaurants without worrying. How I just need to get this assignment done and then I'll feel relaxed.

Surprise! There's always another assignment.

I dream about the day where I've started and sold a business. The day that I make my millions and never have to work again. I feel like I won't be me until I can accomplish that.

What an absurd thing to think. Who will I be the day after that happens? The same exact guy as before.

Knowing that you're more successful than others is a great ego boost. You can walk into the same parties you've been attending and suddenly feel like the man of the hour. But despite all the congratulations in the world, you're still the same person. You're still the guy who isn't satisfied. You might seem momentarily happy, but in your mind, you're still craving more.

I catch myself having these fantasies. I catch myself speeding through my day, mindlessly checking tasks off my to-do list telling myself this is what it takes to be successful. I tell myself these are the things I NEED to do, even if they aren't fun.

When I catch myself, I realize that my accomplishments won't change me. I'll still have the same thoughts on the way to class tomorrow and on the way to work next year.

This is a sobering realization. It's a realization that today is a perfect day if you want it to be. It's believing that you've already accomplished enough. It's a realization that today you are your best you.

It's painfully hard. It's scary having no place to hide and no contingencies on your happiness. But you have no choice. Your only choice is to believe in yourself right now. You can't wait until some external indicator tells you that it's time to start believing. There's no use in waiting, because you'll never feel differently unless you decide to start.

Live the life that you would if you weren't bound by jumping through the next hoop.

You will always be you. Celebrate that because you're the best you there is.

Be Careful of "More"

If you're not happy with what you have, you'll never be happy with what you get.

There are ALWAYS more people to change. You would love to help more families, raise more money, save more lives and empower more children. You have to be careful not to get lost in this mentality of always focusing on more. You are a finite being with limited attention and resources.

If you spend your attention always looking for more people, you lose touch with the magic you created. Be grateful for the people you've already impacted. You must be happy with what you have, because if you can't do that, you will never find happiness in getting one more person in the door.

What We've Covered

- You will always be you
- Happiness is a choice and a skill
- You have already accomplished enough
- If you aren't happy with what you have, you'll never be happy with what you get

10

LIFE IS TOO HARD TO BEAT YOURSELF UP

Life is hard. There is a lot of work to be done and there's always room for improvement. Beating yourself up doesn't help you with any of that.

Develop your self-coach, practice mindfulness and build the strength you need to start living a happier life.

The Myth of Your Self-Critic

There is a myth I quietly told myself for years. Most of the time I didn't even realize it was there. It was so ingrained in my mindset that I couldn't see it.

I would play in a soccer game and complete dozens of passes, but after the game, all I remembered were the few times I gave the ball away. If I scored one goal, I was disappointed that I messed up the other shot I had. After everything I did, I would analyze what didn't work and what needed to be better. There was always something wrong.

As high-achieving people, we tell ourselves the myth that beating ourselves up is healthy. We tell ourselves that this "self-reflection" is the only way to get better. If we thought we were good enough, we'd have no reason to keep working. We believe the negative emotions of self-criticism are a necessary step along the journey of self-improvement.

It's a myth.

There is a better way. The healthier path is to believe you're good enough right now. This confuses people—if you thought you were good enough, what reason would you have to get better? This notion baffled me for a while until one day I realized this:

Improving is inherently enjoyable.

It's just fun to see yourself making progress. Even if it's not toward a specific outcome, the process of self-improvement is its own goal! This means it's possible to believe you're good enough and still get better. That's how we should approach our work.

This shift is not easy to make, though. It requires the crucial skill of non-judgmental observation. You must be able to recognize what could be improved without judging those traits as flaws and errors. They are stepping-stones to improvement, not inherently bad decisions.

You love your favorite band for their music, not for their weird flaws and the bad decisions they've made. Love yourself this same way. Appreciate the good and acknowledge the bad, but don't dwell on it.

Your self-critic is not the reason you're good at anything. You don't need your self-critic. The world has enough critics and there is no reason to create another. Instead, create a self-coach. Invent a productive inner dialogue by coaching yourself to success. Let the voice guide you by supporting you and staying with you each step of the way.

You are your own biggest fan. But if that just doesn't feel like something you can believe right now, know that I believe in you. You're better than you think you are.

Leave the critic behind. Find your inner coach and you're on your way to a great journey.

WE CAN BE GOOD ENOUGH
AND STILL GET BETTER.
PROGRESS FEELS GOOD.

I Was Always Stressed and Never Knew It

The wake up call I needed came in an unexpected form: I was losing my teeth. Not full teeth, but parts of them were chipping. In the middle of the night, my jaw would clench and my teeth ground together. After years of unconsciously doing this, parts of my teeth were gone. The cause of my bad habit? Stress.

I didn't feel stressed, though. I had everything under control all the time. I prided myself on being busy and juggling dozens of activities. Why shouldn't I be proud? I was doing well in school, I started a program, led a club and was busy every day! From the outside everything looked ideal.

On the inside, I was constantly stressed. So much so that I couldn't even sleep without my body finding another outlet to relieve it. I needed a way out. I needed to calm down and get to a more relaxed state.

Meanwhile, I was a huge fan of Tim Ferriss's podcast where he interviews top performers across a variety of disciplines. He talks to actors, entrepreneurs and athletes to tease out the habits that make them world-class. After interviewing over one hundred people, he found that more than 80% of them have some meditation practice. I decided it was finally my time to try it.

I started using apps like Headspace and Calm. After a few weeks of doing 10 minutes each day, I noticed a huge difference in my mood on days when I meditated. When I didn't meditate, I felt rushed. I was moving quickly, forgetting things and being rude to those around me. After a good meditation, I felt ready to take on the day as it came to me. I still felt too busy, but despite having 20 items on my to-do list, I was more relaxed knowing they'd get done eventually. I was still a productive person; I just didn't feel the need to optimize my life to the last second.

After months of meditating and reading several books on the topic, I finally felt the pressure lifting. This feeling is scary because we've been taught all our lives that pressure makes diamonds. When we relax the pressure it seems we might lose our edge.

Fortunately, this isn't true, and it's certainly not an excuse for never trying to meditate. Some of the world's best venture capitalists, CEOs and musicians all practice meditation to keep them performing at their highest levels. In listening to hundreds of these stories, it's clear that no one has lost her edge because she started meditating.

Meditating has never made someone a worse person.

Meditation is a tool that anyone can use. If you don't identify with sitting cross-legged and chanting a mantra, explore other forms of practice. There are dozens of ways to start meditating and each person will have a unique preference. Don't stop all together because one way didn't work. Try a different approach and you'll soon find meditation will help you get to a new level where you'll become a better version of yourself.

Mindfulness Holds It All Together

Happiness is about enjoying the process and appreciating the present moment, but this is not the mindset we've been taught to have. We learned all our lives to be goal-oriented and defer happiness. Reading one book isn't going to change that. This journey will require the discipline to choose happiness each day.

Meditation is a great place to start. Sitting quietly for 10 minutes in the morning and 10 at night will allow your mind to calm down. But, we need to have the right mindset throughout the day in order to start feeling content. For this we need mindfulness.

You know when you open a bag of chips and you look down later to see half the bag is gone and you don't remember tasting any of them? That's the opposite of mindfulness. Trust me, I've done it plenty of times.

It's shocking how often we operate on mindless autopilot. We walk to class failing to see the beautiful trees around us. We read an article unaware that our mind was wandering and we didn't actually read anything. Mindfulness is the practice of staying aware and conscious of what's happening in the present moment. It's appreciating the ground beneath your feet, the feeling of warmth on your skin and the air you breathe.

Mindfulness helps us realize when we're engaging in unnecessary self-criticism. Mindfulness makes us conscious of our insatiable desire for "more." Mindfulness teaches us to take a deep breath and to feel our shoulders drop as our muscles finally relax.

We need to cultivate this practice so we can make mindful choices dozens of times each day. Just like Naval Ravikant said: "Happiness is a choice and a skill." Mindfulness helps us choose happiness in each moment so that we may hone the skill of living happily.

Appreciating the Imperfections

While walking home one winter's night, I had a moment with the world. Instead of being annoyed with how cold my cheeks felt, I thought about the insane scale of what needed to happen in order for me to be alive and feel that sensation. I became grateful that it was there.

The universe was in alignment for me to feel the freezing air.

I had to be present enough to feel this sense of awe. I didn't need to do more. I just needed to slow down and listen.

Cold isn't bad. Our instinct is to think it is, but in reality, cold awakens us. It's nice to feel sometimes.

Every moment is like this. We might think it's bad at first, but really, there is beauty hidden in the struggle. Appreciate the imperfections because they are all you'll ever have.

Choosing Strength

We all want to enjoy life more. There are two choices we have when thinking about how to make it happen: wish the conditions were better, or become more appreciative.

The people who wait for better conditions are those who talk about having fun when they retire. They always have a reason why they're waiting to be happy.

Those who choose appreciation take time for themselves every day. They meditate in the morning, eat well and stay active. They practice gratitude in their daily lives.

"To walk a thorny road, we may cover its every inch with leather or we can make sandals."
— Indian Parable

Which will you choose? Wait for better conditions, or start enjoying life today?

What We've Covered

- You don't need a self-critic to get better
- Meditation will make you less stressed
- Mindfulness helps you find joy in each moment
- Appreciate the imperfections because they are all you'll ever have
- Why wait for better conditions when you can start enjoying life today?

11

THE TIME IS NOW

Why wait? The timing is never more perfect than it is right now. Luckily, you don't need things to be perfect in order to make an impact.

Remember that life is a constant process of becoming. Enjoy the fact that you're not sure what's next. Enjoy the fact that you aren't as successful as you dream to be. Enjoy today because when you're older, you would pay all the money in the world just to be back where you are right now.

This is a beautiful moment and it's the perfect time for you to start changing the world.

Use These Pages as a Reminder

Reminders are important. You're not going to read this book every day, so I encourage you to rip out your favorite pages. Put them up on your wall in a place where you can see them each day. It's easy to get pulled in the wrong direction and fall back to being average because that's what the world wants from you. Keep these pages as a token.

Thank Someone Out of the Blue

As someone making change, you know that it can be a thankless job. It feels like there's no one else that cares and everyone is content staying on the sidelines. But that's just not true. There are countless people putting themselves into their world in a meaningful way. I'm sure you've crossed paths with many of them. Maybe it's a teacher, a coach, a parent, or a boss. They treated you like a human being and believed in your potential. I know who my people were.

There's nothing more powerful than a thank you note out of the blue. I'm sure they feel just like you do sometimes. They're tired and not sure if their impact is landing. Imagine what it would be like to get a note from someone who appreciates them.

It will make their day to hear from you.

ALL JOURNEYS START WITH BELIEF. APPRECIATE THOSE WHO BELIEVED IN YOU AND ALWAYS REMEMBER TO PASS IT ALONG. YOU NEVER KNOW WHO YOU MIGHT INSPIRE TO CHANGE THE WORLD.

MY INSPIRATIONS

Seth Godin, Tim Ferriss, Austin Kleon, David Kadavy, Ramit Sethi, Jonathan Fields, Derek Sivers, Sophia Sadock, Dan Freeman, Ben Rapkin, and my incredible parents